Watchman
Prayer Guide

Linking God's People in Prayer for Spiritual Awakening

LARRY L. THOMPSON

This ministry and study are dedicated to the glory of the Lord Jesus Christ and to the persons who taught me the importance and the power of personal and corporate prayer: James Brown, a dedicated watchman who taught me the prayer of faith, and Cynthia Thompson, who not only taught her husband the value of prayer but also consistently lives the life of a watchman.

© Copyright 1992
Reprinted 1993, 1994, 1996, 1998
LifeWay Press
All rights reserved

ISBN 0-8054-9962-8

The materials provided herein are unrelated to the products and accessories manufactured and sold by Sony Corporation under the trademark WATCH-MAN®, nor is there any sponsorship or relationship with the Sony Corporation.

Printed in United States of America

LifeWay Press
127 Ninth Avenue, North
Nashville, Tennessee 37234

Introduction

For years Christians have known that every great spiritual awakening is born in a remnant committed to prayer. Countless books call people to prayer and emphasize the importance God places on His people's praying. Yet we must answer one sobering question: If prayer is so important, why do most Christians and churches do so little of what God deems essential?

We have more money, more buildings, more ministries, more media, and more people but less power than at any time in church history. We have ministers for every age group. Yet few Christians can claim that they are spiritually stronger today than they were a year ago.

Even churches with outstanding family ministries are not immune to the devastation that a failed marriage brings to their congregations. Our nation boasts some of the finest student ministries, but we remain respectably religious when there is a desperate need for radical relationships with Christ. Single adults compose nearly half of today's population, yet Satan's singles ministry continues to overshadow even our best efforts. We measure the success of our

> **If prayer is so important, why do most Christians and churches do so little of what God deems essential?**

churches in comparison with others, saying, "We are making a difference," but on our best Sunday our combined attendance is dwarfed by the number of unchurched people.

When one considers these facts, an obvious cry grips the heart. There must be more. Where is the power? The answer, quite simply, is that power has always been accessible. We are the ones who have not been available.

Every great spiritual awakening, in our nation and around the world, has had as its foundation a people who were committed to prayer. The Shantung Revival of China came about when Southern Baptist missionaries set themselves apart to pray for the healing of the eyes of one of their own. The Welsh Revival caught fire when a teenage girl cried out to God and proclaimed: "You are everything! You are everything!" The Jesus Movement of the late 1960s and early '70s began on a college campus when students humbly fell before the Lord and prayed.

Today we have the same opportunity for revival. We stand at the door of a passing opportunity at a critical hour in our history. Our response to this call to prayer could determine if we as a people see the glory of God and experience an outpouring of His Spirit on us or if we continue with business as usual: great churches with great fellowship and great people but with little power.

Dilemmas in a church's prayer life have included the logistical difficulties of an organized prayer ministry, such as:

- Driving time to and from locations
- Safety during late-night hours

- Inconvenience for the elderly, for young mothers, and for the handicapped
- Limited number of persons who could participate
- Inclement weather conditions

These problems may result from misplaced theology. In the Old Testament God had a temple for His people, but in the New Testament He had a people for His temple. Many churches have limited the power and significance of prayer to the four walls of the church! We have built elaborate prayer chapels, yet the finest intercessory prayer ministries in our nation have difficulty keeping and maintaining 24-hour ministries. Although we know we need intercessory prayer ministries, most of us have created a structure that is neither practical nor successful.

Our responsibility to be consistent and fruitful in prayer demands that we reevaluate our past methodology and reexamine biblical truth to gain new insights and a fresh model for an intercessory prayer ministry.

Chapter 1: Background

■ The Commissioning of the Watchman

On your walls, O Jerusalem, I have appointed watchmen;
All day and all night they will never keep silent.
You who remind the Lord, take no rest for yourselves;
And give Him no rest until He establishes
And makes Jerusalem a praise in the earth
(Isa. 62:6-7, NASB).[1]

John A. Martin has stated that "in the ancient world watchmen were stationed on city walls"[2] on towers that faced each direction. They were placed there to watch for approaching enemies. Throughout the history of Jerusalem watchmen had a twofold ministry on the wall. The first was to watch for the enemy, providing protection for those asleep or at work. Second, the watchmen were to repair the wall after an attack. At times they would carry out both ministries on the same watch. Because of their extremely important task watchmen were carefully appointed and commissioned. Once they had accepted the position as watchmen, failure to carry out their duties responsibly could result in their own deaths as well as the death of God's work in that city.

■ The Duties of the Watchman
Watchmen took their places on the walls to "remind the Lord" (Isa. 62:6, NASB). The implication is that they were to give neither themselves nor the Lord any rest until He established His presence and power in their midst. Their foremost prayer was "Make us a city of praise on the earth." Additionally, the watchmen had two specific responsibilities:

1. *Watchmen reminded God of His people.* Some might say that God does not need to be reminded of His people. However, children often tell their parents what the parents already know, and both the children and the parents are blessed by the communication, interaction, and dependence shown. As my daughters converse with me, they may share information or experiences I know well, but I rejoice in their desire to share their time and fellowship, which deepen and strengthen our bond of love.

2. *Watchmen reminded God's people of His promises.* The presence of the watchmen stationed around the walls constantly reminded all in the city that they belonged to God. By shouting Scripture and repairing the broken places, they daily confronted the people with the promise of God's protection and love.

■ The Diligence of the Watchman
The Bible indicates that the watchmen were present "all day and all night" (Isa. 62:6, NASB). There was never a time when the walls were not secure and the people silent. The

watchmen made continuous intercession on behalf of all the people. The watchmen were also committed to the personal preparation of their own lives while standing watch, and they corporately prayed for revival and the establishment of Jerusalem. The fact that their voices were constantly heard assured the people of the city that they had "set a watch" to mark the time and to show that they were constantly attentive to their duties. Constant intercession in our midst will encourage those who are going through difficult times, because they know the watchmen are being faithful to make prayerful petitions on behalf of the people.

Chapter 2: Description

Through the Holy Spirit's leadership and a call to the Watchman Ministry, an individual will be assigned one hour a week on the wall in one direction: north, south, east, or west. If only one wall is used, then the directions will not be necessary. Each wall consists of 168 prayer warriors, one for each hour of the day, 7 days a week and 24 hours a day. A watchman will pray toward the direction assigned.

After you have prayerfully committed to the Watchman Ministry, your church will give you instructions on how to register for your assigned hour. You will also need to complete the covenant at the back of this booklet during the worship service on Launch Sunday. Your pastor will instruct you to sign the covenant in that service as all the watchmen in your church join together for a time of dedication and commitment.

Once the hour is assigned, the watchman will "set the watch" for that hour as instructed in *Watchman Prayer Alert,* a monthly newsletter the church mails to all watchmen. *Watchman Prayer Alert* will inform interces-

> **Each wall consists of 168 prayer warriors, one for each hour of the day, 7 days a week and 24 hours a day.**

sors of needs in the church's fellowship and of ministries that require special attention.

Keep in mind the twofold purpose of the Watchman Ministry: (1) to remind the Lord of His promise and covenant with His people, asking for His protection for their lives and ministry, and (2) to remind the people of the Lord's presence and of His provision and protection.

Following the assigned hour on the wall, the watchman will call the next hour's watchman to duty. The watch may take place wherever the intercessor is, as long as one uninterrupted hour to watch and to be with the Lord is available. A list of intercessors and their telephone numbers is made accessible through the Watchman Ministry so the intercessor can phone the person scheduled for the next watch and report: "I have completed my watch of the north wall. I now commend you to the Lord while you watch and pray."

This approach is so simple that reserve intercessors are not needed in case of absences. For instance, if the watchman is out of town, he or she is still accountable for the same hour on the wall and, if possible, for calling the next watchman. Watchmen will continue serving their assigned hours until they notify the prayer office that they wish to be relieved of the responsibility. If an intercessor fails to take the assigned watch, the prayer office will call and offer assistance. If the watchman fails to keep his assigned hour of watch for two consecutive weeks, the prayer office will enlist a replacement.

To secure a position on the wall, a watchman must be of a mature and responsible age.

Parents are encouraged to allow children to participate in the parents' assigned hours on the wall. This will be good training and spiritual preparation for the child, who will understand the principle of prayer through practice with the parents.

Chapter 3: Promise

The Lord makes a twofold commitment to those who answer the call to the wall.

■ His Protection

In Isaiah 62:8 God promised:

> *"I will never again give your grain as food for your enemies;*
> *Nor will foreigners drink your new wine, for which you have labored"* (NASB).

These words demonstrate a unique balance between humans' intercession and God's sovereignty. During the years when Israel had remained silent before the Lord, the enemy had consumed everything for which the Israelites had worked. Their silence was evidence that they had a self-sufficient attitude, having forgotten the Lord's power and provision. Once they accepted their appointment to the wall, God committed to protect them from their enemies. It is obvious today that our congregations' families and singles need this kind of pro-

---

Without God's protection the enemy is allowed to consume us at the point of our need.

tection. Without God's protection we have a problem: The enemy is allowed to consume us at the point of our need, and we get weaker while the enemy gets stronger.

■ His Provision

Once the people respond to God and meet His conditions, not only will the protection from the enemy be present, but also the provision will be bountiful and the needs met. The Lord has promised His harvest to those who obey His call (see Isa. 62:8-9).

Chapter 4: Challenge

■ Your Praise

> "Those who harvest it will eat it
>   and praise the Lord,
> and those who gather the grapes will drink it
>   in the courts of my sanctuary"
>   (Isa. 62:9, NIV).[3]

A natural response of God's people when His provision and protection are realized in their midst is an expression of praise. Much of our work on the walls during the week will be filled with praise as we thank the Father for His protection and provision in our midst. God has made a commitment to us in the form of an oath, and He continues to wait for us to answer the call to the wall and to take our places in the ministry of intercession.

■ Your Preparation

> *Prepare the way for the people.*
> *Build up, build up the highway!*
>   *Remove the stones.*
> *Raise a banner for the nations.*
>
> . . . .
> " 'See, your Savior comes!*
> *See, his reward is with him,*
>   *and his recompense accompanies him' "*
>   (Isa. 62:10-11, NIV).

> **God has made a
> commitment to us
> in the form of an oath.**

As John the Baptist cried in the wilderness and proclaimed, " 'Behold, the Lamb of God who takes away the sin of the world!' " (John 1:29, NASB), we too must proclaim and make straight the path for the Lord's return. We must clear away the debris of sin and slothfulness that would cause others to stumble on their way to meet Jesus. We must prepare the way by lifting high the banner of our King for all to see. We must act! In doing so, we have the assurance that the world will recognize God's people. Our prayer on the walls will usher in a spiritual awakening in our church that will arouse our community and eventually the world. We stand at a crossroads with the privilege of preparing the way for the Lord and then being proclaimed as His people.

■ Your Position

> *They will be called the Holy People,
>   the Redeemed of the Lord;
> and you will be called Sought After,
>   the City No Longer Deserted*
>   (Isa. 62:12, NIV).

Notice that the Scripture says, "They will be called. . . ." This means that the world will take notice. Because God's people have answered the call to the wall and have set their watch with God, the world cannot avoid noticing His power, protection, and provision for His people. You will be called "the Holy People, the Redeemed of the Lord . . . Sought After, the City No Longer Deserted" (v. 12, NIV).

Our call is now! Each day that we fail to answer God's call to intercessory prayer, another family is broken apart, another teenager is lost to suicide, another job is lost, another financial collapse is witnessed, another day passes during which our nation moves closer to a date with destruction. I beg you to answer this call to the wall. If not for our nation, if not for the sea of humanity that is lost and bound for eternity in hell, if not for your church that stands as a lighthouse in this explosive community, if not for any other reason, would you take your hour for yourself and for those you love? The walls are silent today; they await your appointment.

Chapter 5: Instructions

Leonard Ravenhill has said, "One might estimate the weight of the world, tell the size of the celestial city, count the stars of heaven, measure the speed of lightning, and tell the time of the rising and the setting of the sun–but you cannot estimate prayer-power. Prayer is as vast as God because He is behind it. Prayer is as mighty as God because He has committed Himself to answer it."[4]

After you have been appointed to the Watchman Ministry and have been assigned your hour and your direction, you will be ready to prepare yourself for your ministry in prayer. Follow these simple preparatory steps.

1. **Take your position a few minutes before your assigned watch.** The watchman before you should phone and commend you to the Lord for your watch. However, if you do not receive a call, begin your watch on the assigned hour. If you fail to receive a call from the previous watchman for two consecutive weeks, alert the office coordinating the prayer ministry so an inquiry can be made.

> "You cannot estimate prayer-power. Prayer is as vast as God because He is behind it."

2. **As you begin your watch, use this checklist to make sure you are ready to pray.**

   - *Are all sins confessed?* (See Isa. 59:1-2; 1 John 1:10.)
   - *Are relationships with all others right?* (See Matt. 6:14-15.)
   - *Are you prepared to seek His will in all things?* (See 1 John 5:14-15.)
   - *Are you willing to allow God to receive all glory?* (See John 14:13-14.)
   - *Are you depending on the Holy Spirit's leadership for this watch on the wall?* (See Rom. 8:26-27.)
   - *Are you trusting in God in spite of the circumstances?* (See Prov. 3:5-6.)
   - *Are you willing to praise the Lord in all things?* (See Rom. 8:28; 1 Thess. 5:16-18.)

3. **Follow the instructions in this month's *Watchman Prayer Alert.***

4. **Remember that you are charged with the watch for the entire hour.**

5. **Your last prayer before ending your hour on the wall should be for the watchman who is following you on the wall.** Call the person by name and ask for the Lord's encouragement in his or her life.

6. **As you finish your hour, phone the next watchman and remind him or her of the watch.** Make your message simple and to the point. For example, greet the person and

say: "I have completed the watch on the north wall, and now I commend you to the Lord for your watch. May God bless you as He has blessed me." If you cannot reach this watchman for two consecutive weeks, call the office coordinating the prayer ministry so an inquiry can be made.

7. **Take a moment and record any thoughts, answered prayers, or claimed promises in the Watchman Journal section of this guide.** A simple sentence with a date will give you and your family a point of reference later to remember what God has done in your lives.

8. **If you have any questions or need to make any changes in your assigned hour on the wall, call the office coordinating the prayer ministry.**

9. **Remember that Satan will do all he can to keep you from your watch.** You must be "strong in the Lord, and in the strength of His might" (Eph. 6:10, NASB). Our authority is useless unless it is used!

The Watchman Journal

Almost every Christian leader at some time has encouraged believers to learn the discipline of journaling. By keeping a journal of your experience as a watchman, you will learn to blend your spiritual journey with your daily walk.

To understand the value of journaling, think of using your journal as a spiritual diary. The pages provided for you in this booklet are by no means intended to be all you will need to describe your walk with God. However, they will allow you to keep a weekly record of how the Lord has met you in your hour on the wall. You may want to record prayer requests, answered prayers, Bible promises, spiritual direction, or simply your personal thoughts while in the Lord's presence.

Furthermore, the journal will help you chart your spiritual progress through the year. It will help you hold yourself accountable for God's instructions during your times of prayer. You can read the journal of David's spiritual pilgrimage in the Psalms. There you will find that some days were filled with victory, praise, and thanksgiving. However, you will also find the transparent writings of a man who was at times discouraged and defeated. The beauty of those times is that David's journal ultimately leads to victory through his relationship with God.

Each week's material in the journal provides a Scripture passage that is intended to encourage you as you begin your hour. Read the verse and meditate on what the Lord is teaching you through His Word. As you read and pray, be open to the direction of God's Spirit. At the conclusion of your prayer hour take a moment to record your thoughts or impressions that resulted from your time with the Lord.

The most important factor is your consistency. As you pray and enter your journal record, you will find periodic pages of encouragement called Rest Stops. The progress of your prayer life is like any journey. As you make progress, you will find signs encouraging you to stop for rest and renewal before you continue. The Rest Stops in the journal will provide you the spiritual refreshment needed to complete your walk and commitment.

Now you are ready to begin this journey. Be sure to practice the discipline of journaling. You will find it a fruitful, rewarding experience as you maintain your persistence and consistency.

Week 1 Date _____

My prayer is not for them alone. I pray also for those who will believe in me through their message.
            John 17:20, NIV

Week 2 Date _____

May your eyes be open toward this temple night and day, this place of which you said, "My Name shall be there," so that you will hear the prayer your servant prays toward this place.
            1 Kings 8:29, NIV

Week 3 Date _____

*The eyes of the Lord are on the righteous
    and his ears are attentive to their prayer,
but the face of the Lord is against those who do evil.*
            1 Peter 3:12, NIV

Week 4 Date ―――――

Confess your sins to each other and pray for each other so that you may be healed. The prayer of a righteous man is powerful and effective.

James 5:16, NIV

Week 5 Date ―――――

Give attention to your servant's prayer and his plea for mercy, O Lord my God. Hear the cry and the prayer that your servant is praying in your presence. 2 Chronicles 6:19, NIV

Week 6 Date ―――――

I want men everywhere to lift up holy hands in prayer, without anger or disputing.

1 Timothy 2:8, NIV

JOURNAL

Week 7 Date _____

Hear from heaven their prayer and their plea, and uphold their cause.
  2 Chronicles 6:35, NIV

Week 8 Date _____

Devote yourselves to prayer, being watchful and thankful. Colossians 4:2, NIV

Week 9 Date _____

May your eyes be open toward this temple day and night, this place of which you said you would put your Name there. May you hear the prayer your servant prays toward this place.
  2 Chronicles 6:20, NIV

Gas, Food, and Water

REST STOP

Anyone who has ever taken a journey with children knows the value of periodic stops. Some can go longer than others, but eventually we all need to stop to rest, refuel, and replenish!

Sometimes in the Christian walk we start to lose perspective and tire of doing what is essential to our effectiveness. During that time we tend to move from spiritual power to personal reserve. Once we start trying to make spiritual progress in our own strength, we begin to grow weary and discouraged.

At those times we need to stop to rest and refuel. When Moses took time to be alone with God, he quickly recognized the value of personal prayer and solitude. Several times in Scripture we read that Jesus rose early in the morning and went out alone to pray. If Jesus needed to stop from the pressure of life and responsibilities, why would we think we could do less? If the Creator needed to rest, then His creation should realize the value of rest. Don't underestimate this weekly time alone with God. You can run on empty only so long before the engine shuts down and the progress stops. Be encouraged: a rest stop is ahead. Plan now to rest, refuel, and go forward!

Week 10 Date _____

This is my prayer: that your love may abound more and more in knowledge and depth of insight. Philippians 1:9, NIV

Week 11 Date _____

Since the day we heard about you, we have not stopped praying for you and asking God to fill you with the knowledge of his will through all spiritual wisdom and understanding.
Colossians 1:9, NIV

Week 12 Date _____

O Lord, let your ear be attentive to the prayer of this your servant and to the prayer of your servants who delight in revering your name.
Nehemiah 1:11, NIV

Week 13   Date

From heaven, your dwelling place, hear their prayer and their pleas, and uphold their cause. And forgive your people, who have sinned against you.

2 Chronicles 6:39, NIV

Week 14   Date

Do not be anxious about anything, but in everything, by prayer and petition, with thanksgiving, present your requests to God.

Philippians 4:6, NIV

Week 15   Date

We fasted and petitioned our God about this, and he answered our prayer.

Ezra 8:23, NIV

JOURNAL

Week 16   Date _____

I call on you, O God, for you will answer me;
*   give ear to me and hear my prayer.*
                              Psalm 17:6, NIV

Week 17   Date _____

The priests and the Levites stood to bless the people, and God heard them, for their prayer reached heaven, his holy dwelling place.
                            2 Chronicles 30:27, NIV

Week 18   Date _____

Be joyful in hope, patient in affliction, faithful in prayer.
                                Romans 12:12, NIV

Rough Road Ahead

Too often Christian pilgrims have a difficult time making it through a wilderness experience. Perhaps these first 18 weeks of prayer have been difficult, and you are somewhat discouraged by the journey so far. Remember that the wilderness does not have to mean utter hopelessness and despair. God has a perfect plan for us even in difficult times. The children of Israel matured and learned obedience and dependence on the Lord during their days in the wilderness. Moses spent 40 years in the desert learning that he did not have to solve in his own strength every problem that came his way but instead that he could rely on God's power and provision. Jesus also experienced days of discouragement. In the wilderness He learned to seek the Scriptures in times of turmoil and distress, and He left the wilderness in victory.

Too often Christians try to take a detour around a rough road. Remember, to bypass the wilderness on our way to the promised land would be to bypass God and His provision and protection.

REST STOP

Week 19 Date _____

*The Lord has heard my cry for mercy;
the Lord accepts my prayer.*
Psalm 6:9, NIV

Week 20 Date _____

Paul and Barnabas appointed elders for them in each church and, with prayer and fasting, committed them to the Lord, in whom they had put their trust. Acts 14:23, NIV

Week 21 Date _____

*As he taught them, he said, "Is it not written:
'My house will be called
 a house of prayer for all nations'?
But you have made it 'a den of robbers.'"*
Mark 11:17, NIV

Week 22 Date _____

They devoted themselves to the apostles' teaching and to the fellowship, to the breaking of bread and to prayer.

Acts 2:42, NIV

Week 23 Date _____

*Answer me when I call to you,
 O my righteous God.
Give me relief from my distress;
 be merciful to me and hear my prayer.*
Psalm 4:1, NIV

Week 24 Date _____

If you believe, you will receive whatever you ask for in prayer. Matthew 21:22, NIV

JOURNAL

Week 25　　　　　　　Date

*The Lord is far from the wicked
　but he hears the prayer of the righteous.*
　　　　　　　　　　　Proverbs 15:29, NIV

Week 26　　　　　　　Date

*O Lord, hear my prayer,
　listen to my cry for mercy;
in your faithfulness and righteousness
　come to my relief.*

　　　　　　　　　　　　Psalm 143:1, NIV

Week 27　　　　　　　Date

Is any one of you in trouble? He should pray. Is anyone happy? Let him sing songs of praise.
　　　　　　　　　　　　James 5:13, NIV

Scenic Turnout Ahead

While traveling on vacation, I was captivated by a sign that instructed, "Scenic Turnout 1 Mile Ahead." The pressure of trying to meet the day's schedule almost caused me to pass this opportunity. At the last minute I decided to take the time to view the scenery hidden by the road. Less than one hundred yards away was the most breathtaking view of God's natural creation that I had ever seen.

When I recall that experience and realize that I came within a second of passing by the beauty, I shudder at the thought of almost losing that opportunity. How many times on life's journey has God encouraged us to stop and take time to examine the Creator's beauty? The scenic turnout in your life could be spending time with your spouse, taking a walk with the children, calling an aged relative and giving a word of encouragement, taking a walk around the block, meeting a new neighbor, or visiting a hospital.

Life's pace is faster than that of the interstate. What a tragedy for the Christian to speed through life never taking time for the scenic turnout. How long has it been since you got off life's highway to walk down the path of solitude with the Savior?

Week 28 Date _____

*These I will bring to my holy mountain
  and give them joy in my house of prayer.
Their burnt offerings and sacrifices
  will be accepted on my altar;
for my house will be called
  a house of prayer for all nations.*
                                    Isaiah 56:7, NIV

Week 29 Date _____

*O Lord, hear my prayer,
  listen to my cry for mercy;
in your faithfulness and righteousness
  come to my relief.*   Psalm 143:1, NIV

Week 30 Date _____

Pray for us that the message of the Lord may spread rapidly and be honored, just as it was with you.   2 Thessalonians 3:1, NIV

Week 31 Date _____

As for me, far be it from me that I should sin against the Lord by failing to pray for you. And I will teach you the way that is good and right.
1 Samuel 12:23, NIV

Week 32 Date _____

We pray this in order that you may live a life worthy of the Lord and may please him in every way: bearing fruit in every good work, growing in the knowledge of God.

Colossians 1:10, NIV

Week 33 Date _____

Now we pray to God that you will not do anything wrong. Not that people will see that we have stood the test but that you will do what is right even though we may seem to have failed.
2 Corinthians 13:7, NIV

Week 34 Date _____

If my people, who are called by my name, will humble themselves and pray and seek my face and turn from their wicked ways, then will I hear from heaven and will forgive their sin and will heal their land.

2 Chronicles 7:14, NIV

Week 35 Date _____

Pray in the Spirit on all occasions with all kinds of prayers and requests. With this in mind, be alert and always keep on praying for all the saints. Ephesians 6:18, NIV

Week 36 Date _____

On reaching the place, he said to them, "Pray that you will not fall into temptation."
Luke 22:40, NIV

Slippery When Wet

How many times on the highway of life have you come across this sign? It warns the traveler that a safe road could be transformed into a dangerous one with a slight change in weather conditions.

If you fail to respond to the warnings, you could find yourself in a ditch with damage to you as well as to your mode of transportation. In our Christian journey our adversary is constantly erecting obstacles that would cause the children of God to slip. It is imperative that we watch the road and heed the warnings the Word of God provides. As you take time for this rest stop, ask yourself, *Has God placed any warning signs in my path that I need to heed so I can alter my course to prevent damage to me and those I love?* If your answer is yes, remember that He places His warnings in our path for one reason: to protect those He loves.

JOURNAL

Week 37 Date _____

Give attention to your servant's prayer and his plea for mercy, O Lord my God. Hear the cry and the prayer that your servant is praying in your presence this day. 1 Kings 8:28, NIV

Week 38 Date _____

One day Jesus was praying in a certain place. When he finished, one of his disciples said to him, "Lord, teach us to pray, just as John taught his disciples." Luke 11:1, NIV

Week 39 Date _____

In the same way, the Spirit helps us in our weakness. We do not know what we ought to pray for, but the Spirit himself intercedes for us with groans that words cannot express.
Romans 8:26, NIV

Week 40 Date _____

It may be that the Lord your God will hear the words of the field commander . . . and that he will rebuke him for the words the Lord your God has heard. Therefore pray for the remnant that still survives. Isaiah 37:4, NIV

Week 41 Date _____

Be always on the watch, and pray that you may be able to escape all that is about to happen, and that you may be able to stand before the Son of Man. Luke 21:36, NIV

Week 42 Date _____

"Why are you sleeping?" he asked them. "Get up and pray so that you will not fall into temptation."

Luke 22:46, NIV

Week 43 Date _____

I pray also that the eyes of your heart may be enlightened in order that you may know the hope to which he has called you, the riches of his glorious inheritance in the saints.
                              Ephesians 1:18, NIV

Week 44 Date _____

Give attention to your servant's prayer and his plea for mercy, O Lord my God. Hear the cry and the prayer that your servant is praying in your presence.   2 Chronicles 6:19, NIV

Week 45 Date _____

When you stand praying, if you hold anything against anyone, forgive him, so that your Father in heaven may forgive you your sins.
                                  Mark 11:25, NIV

Detour Ahead

I don't know anyone who likes to see a detour sign in the middle of a journey. It slows the trip; the roads are never as smooth as the main road; and the 10 miles of construction seem that they will never end!

Life is like the Road Under Construction sign. Every Christian has periods when the Lord decides that it is time to make necessary repairs. At times those repairs are painful, time-consuming, emotionally draining, and seemingly never-ending.

The truth is that these times end, and when they do, we are better because we went through the experience and allowed the Lord to complete His perfect work in our lives. The process will result in a much smoother and more efficient ride through the journey we call life.

One time I ignored a detour sign and tried to continue on the highway being repaired. Two flats, one torn shirt, and a lost temper later, I returned to take the proper detour. There is never a shortcut when traveling on the highway of life. If you find yourself in one of those under-construction periods, rejoice. It won't last forever!

Week 46 Date _____

One of those days Jesus went out to a mountainside to pray, and spent the night praying to God.
Luke 6:12, NIV

Week 47 Date _____

You, dear friends, build yourselves up in your most holy faith and pray in the Holy Spirit.
Jude 20, NIV

Week 48 Date _____

*Hear my prayer, O Lord;
listen to my cry for mercy.*
Psalm 86:6, NIV

Week 49 Date _____

Hear from heaven, your dwelling place, and when you hear, forgive.

1 Kings 8:30, NIV

Week 50 Date _____

I pray that you may be active in sharing your faith, so that you will have a full understanding of every good thing we have in Christ.

Philemon 6, NIV

Week 51 Date _____

Pray continually.

1 Thessalonians 5:17, NIV

JOURNAL

Week 52   Date _____

When Solomon finished praying, fire came down from heaven and consumed the burnt offering and the sacrifices, and the glory of the Lord filled the temple.

2 Chronicles 7:1, NIV

Home at Last!

The best part of the journey is coming home. It has been a year since you made your commitment to join the Watchman Prayer Ministry. As you review your journal, use it as you would a photo album of a recent trip. The memories will encourage you as you realize how the Lord has graciously brought you through the year and has given you victory through this journey. Congratulations on completing the trip.

REST STOP

Notes

[1] From the *New American Standard Bible*. © The Lockman Foundation, 1960, 1962, 1963, 1968, 1971, 1972, 1973, 1975, 1977. Used by permission. Subsequent quotations are marked NASB.

[2] John A. Martin, *The Bible Knowledge Commentary*, ed. John F. Walvoord and Roy B. Zuck (Wheaton: Victor Books, 1985), 1117.

[3] From the Holy Bible, *New International Version*, copyright © 1973, 1978, 1984 by International Bible Society. Subsequent quotations are marked NIV.

[4] Leonard Ravenhill, *Illustrations Unlimited*, ed. James S. Hewett (Wheaton: Tyndale House Publishers, Inc., 1988), 424-25.

Record the following information here for quick reference. Use a pencil in case of changes.

Name _____

Address _____

Phone _____

My watchman hour _____

Church-prayer-line number _____

Watchman who precedes me _____

Phone _____

Watchman who follows me _____

Phone _____

Watchman Prayer Ministry Covenant

After careful consideration and much prayer, I know that the Lord is leading me to commit myself to becoming a prayer warrior in the Watchman Prayer Ministry.

I understand that I will commit one hour a week for one year as I join other watchmen to pray for revival and spiritual awakening. I make this covenant that I will faithfully take my hour in prayer and will intercede for revival and spiritual awakening. Each week I will also call the watchman who follows me on the wall and will pray as that person begins his or her watch.

Finally, I ask the Lord to mature me and strengthen me as I fulfill my commitment. I eagerly accept my hour on the wall and await the challenge, power, and blessing that come from the ministry of prayer.

Name ───────────────────

Be prepared to sign the covenant during the worship service on Launch Sunday.